MARYLAND

HELLO
U.S.A.

by Joyce Johnston

Lerner Publications Company

S

STATES
MARYLAND

You'll find this picture of oysters at the beginning of each chapter in this book. Marylanders have fished for oysters in Chesapeake Bay for hundreds of years. Fishers use a tool called a dredge to scrape oysters off the bottom of the bay. Some oysters are sold fresh, and many others are canned. Maryland fishers harvest an average of 2 million oysters each year.

Cover (left): Graduating midshipmen at the United States Naval Academy in Annapolis. Cover (right): Steamed crabs near an Annapolis marina. Pages 2–3: A lighthouse on Chesapeake Bay. Page 3: Downtown Annapolis.

Copyright © 2003 by Lerner Publications Company

This book is available in two editions:
Library binding by Lerner Publications Company, a division of Lerner Publishing Group
Soft cover by First Avenue Editions, an imprint of Lerner Publishing Group
241 First Avenue North
Minneapolis, MN 55401 U.S.A.

Website address: www.lernerbooks.com

Library of Congress Cataloging-in-Publication Data

Johnston, Joyce, 1958–
    Maryland / by Joyce Johnston (Rev. and expanded 2nd ed.)
      p.   cm. — (Hello U.S.A.)
    Includes bibliographical references and index.
    ISBN: 0–8225–4094–0 (lib. bdg. : alk. paper)
    ISBN: 0–8225–0782–X (pbk. : alk. paper)
    1. Maryland—Juvenile literature. [1. Maryland.] I. Title. II. Series.
  F181.3 .J64 2003   2001007212

Manufactured in the United States of America
1 2 3 4 5 6 – JR – 08 07 06 05 04 03

CONTENTS

A waterman's workboat rests at a small boat dock on Tilghman Island, in Chesapeake Bay.

THE LAND

Chesapeake Country

he Chesapeake Bay is a long, narrow arm of the Atlantic Ocean. It cuts deep into the East Coast of the United States, lapping against the cliffs and beaches of Maryland and Virginia. The bay cuts far north into Maryland, slicing the state nearly in two.

Maryland, the eighth smallest state in the nation, is a southern state. The Mason-Dixon Line—the historical boundary between the North and the South—divides Maryland from its northern neighbor, Pennsylvania. Maryland has a winding southern border, created mostly by the Potomac River. South of the Potomac lie Virginia and West Virginia. Delaware and the Atlantic Ocean are Maryland's neighbors to the east.

Ducks, swans, and other waterfowl spend winters along the Chesapeake Bay.

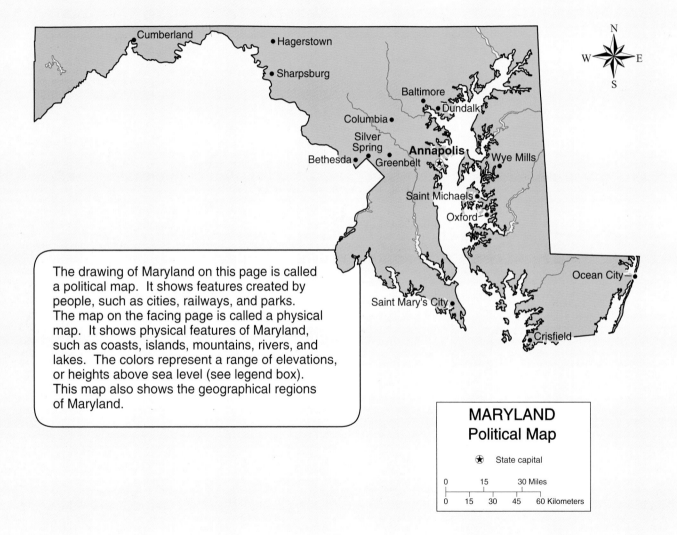

Cumberland

Hagerstown

Sharpsburg

Baltimore

Dundalk

Columbia

Silver
Spring

Annapolis

Bethesda

Greenbelt

Wye Mills

Saint Michaels

Oxford

Saint Mary's City

Ocean City

Crisfield

The drawing of Maryland on this page is called
a political map. It shows features created by
people, such as cities, railways, and parks.
The map on the facing page is called a physical
map. It shows physical features of Maryland,
such as coasts, islands, mountains, rivers, and
lakes. The colors represent a range of elevations,
or heights above sea level (see legend box).
This map also shows the geographical regions
of Maryland.

MARYLAND
Political Map

⭐ State capital

0   15   30 Miles

0   15   30   45   60 Kilometers

8

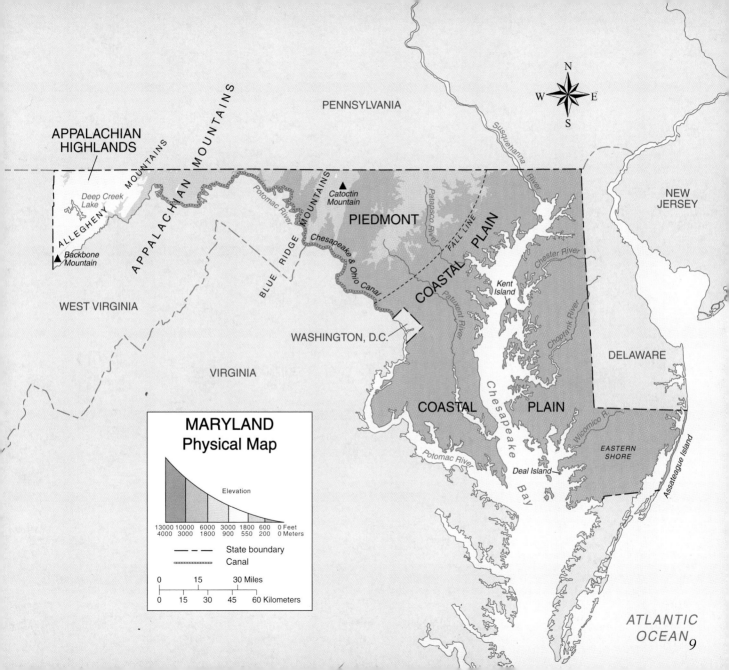

MARYLAND
Physical Map

Elevation

| 13000 | 10000 | 6000 | 3000 | 1800 | 600 | 0 Feet |
| 4000 | 3000 | 1800 | 900 | 550 | 200 | 0 Meters |

— — — State boundary

┅┅┅ Canal

0   15   30 Miles

0 15 30 45 60 Kilometers

APPALACHIAN
HIGHLANDS

PENNSYLVANIA

Deep Creek
Lake

APPALACHIAN MOUNTAINS

ALLEGHENY MOUNTAINS

Potomac River

Catoctin
Mountain

PIEDMONT

Patapsco River

Susquehanna River

FALL LINE

COASTAL PLAIN

NEW
JERSEY

Backbone
Mountain

APPALACHIAN MOUNTAINS

BLUE RIDGE MOUNTAINS

Chesapeake & Ohio Canal

Chester River

Kent
Island

Patuxent River

Choptank River

WEST VIRGINIA

WASHINGTON, D.C.

DELAWARE

VIRGINIA

COASTAL   PLAIN

Wicomico R.

EASTERN
SHORE

Potomac River

Deal Island

Chesapeake Bay

Assateague Island

ATLANTIC
OCEAN 9

N
W   E
S

Calvert Cliffs *(above right)*, on the west side of Chesapeake Bay, is a favorite spot for fossil hunting. Tall grasses *(inset)* are abundant in Maryland's wetlands.

Maryland has three land regions—the Coastal Plain, the Piedmont, and the Appalachian Highlands. The Coastal Plain stretches across eastern Maryland on both sides of the Chesapeake Bay. The land east of the bay is called the Eastern Shore. The plain gradually rises from flatlands to low hills. **Marshes**, or wetlands, line the bay. Pine forests are found throughout the plain.

The Piedmont region stretches across the middle of Maryland from north to south. Low, wooded hills rise gently from the region's wide valleys. Dairy farms, as well as fields of wheat and corn, are common sights in the Piedmont.

The Appalachian Highlands rise beyond the Piedmont in the westernmost part of the state.

The Piedmont region is home to many dairy farms.

Oak leaves and moss color the forest floor at Catoctin Mountain Park near the Appalachian Trail.

Two mountain ranges, the Alleghenies and the Blue Ridge, cross the highlands. Their steep ridges and peaks are part of the Appalachian Mountains, an ancient mountain chain that stretches all the way from Canada to Alabama. The Blue Ridge Mountains are named for the blue haze that hangs over the mountain forests. Backbone Mountain, a peak of the Alleghenies, rises to 3,360 feet. It is the tallest point in Maryland.

Not far from Backbone Mountain lie the quiet waters of Deep Creek Lake, the largest lake in Maryland. Deep Creek, like all lakes in Maryland, is artificial. People created the lake by damming up a river.

More than 50 rivers flow through Maryland to the Chesapeake Bay. The Potomac, Patuxent, and

The Chesapeake Bay shoreline is broken up by lots of rivers, bays, and islands.

Patapsco Rivers run through the western part of the state. The Susquehanna, in northeastern Maryland, brings water into the Chesapeake from as far away as New York. The Chester and Choptank Rivers wind their way through the forests, farmlands, and marshes of the Eastern Shore.

The streams and rivers that flow across western Maryland toward the Chesapeake Bay cross a boundary called the Fall Line. This boundary separates the Piedmont from the Coastal Plain. As the streams and rivers tumble over the Fall Line, they form waterfalls and rapids.

The Chesapeake Bay and the Atlantic Ocean affect weather conditions in the Coastal Plain. In summer the waters absorb heat, cooling the land around them. In the winter, the waters act like huge radiators, giving back the heat collected in summer and warming the land nearby. Farther from

Maryland's forests are spectacular in fall, when the leaves turn brilliant colors.

the water, the Piedmont and the Appalachians have different weather patterns. These regions tend to be cooler than the Coastal Plain in winter. Summers can be hot and humid all over the state.

The mild winters of the Eastern Shore attract many kinds of birds to Maryland. Nearly 1 million ducks and geese from the northern United States and Canada spend winters in Maryland's marshy areas. During winter and summer, oysters, crabs, and clams live in the bay. White-tailed deer, raccoons, red and gray foxes, and opossums roam the state's forests year-round.

Forests cover almost half of Maryland. Loblolly pine, sweet gum, Spanish oak, and bald cypress trees grow near the wetlands in southern Maryland. In the northwest, evergreen trees such as white pines and hemlocks fill the cool mountain forests.

Maryland's state flower is the black-eyed Susan.

The Old Line State

 n almost any map of Maryland, you can find traces of the first peoples who lived there. Chesapeake, Wicomico, Catoctin, Allegheny, Assateague—all of these and many more of Maryland's place-names come from Native American, or Indian, words.

Indians probably came to North America from Asia about 10,000 years ago. Eventually, some Indians reached the area that later became Maryland. These people didn't live in cities and towns. They moved from place to place, hunting deer and looking for other sources of food.

Later, Indians built small houses called lodges. They set traps to catch animals. They fished the rivers and the Chesapeake Bay with nets, sinkers, and

hooks. The Indians also traded food and blankets with neighboring groups to the north and south.

By the late 1500s, several Indian nations were living near the Chesapeake Bay. The Piscataway made their homes in southern Maryland. The Nanticoke, Choptank, Assateague, and Pocomoke had territories on the Eastern Shore. The Susquehanna settled at the top of the bay.

Native Americans in the Maryland area built homes known as lodges.

Around this time, explorers from Europe crossed the Atlantic Ocean and landed on the shores of North America. Pedro Menéndez de Avilés, a Spanish sea captain, traveled to Florida in 1565. He later explored the Chesapeake Bay. John Smith, an English explorer, sailed up the bay into Maryland in 1608. In 1631 William Claiborne established a trading post on Kent Island in the bay.

In 1632 the king of Britain, Charles I, granted part of the Chesapeake Bay area to a British nobleman, Lord Baltimore. The king named this land Mariland (later spelled Maryland) after his wife, Queen Henrietta Maria.

Maryland was named for England's Queen Henrietta Maria.

This painting shows Native Americans greeting Maryland's first British settlers.

Lord Baltimore planned to start a **colony**, or settlement, of British people in Maryland. In the spring of 1634, two British ships sailed into the Chesapeake Bay and up the Potomac River. They carried about 150 people who wanted to make Maryland their new home.

Maryland's colonists found a natural harbor— a place where ships could dock easily—along the Potomac River. The newcomers built houses, a fort, and a church near the harbor. They called their new settlement Saint Mary's City.

Among the settlers was Leonard Calvert, one of Lord Baltimore's sons. Calvert became the colony's first governor. He allowed people to choose their own religion—a freedom they did not have in Britain. Because Calvert permitted freedom of religion, people from other North American colonies and more people from Britain flocked to Maryland.

Leonard Calvert greets an Indian aboard the *Ark,* one of two ships that carried settlers to Maryland.

Many Indians were friendly to the British settlers, trading furs and food for tools and cloth. The Indians taught the newcomers how to plant corn, a skill that saved the settlers from starvation. To make sure they would have food during the winter, the settlers worked hard planting crops in spring.

Some farmers planted tobacco, used in making cigarettes and cigars. Dried tobacco leaves were sold to Great Britain. With the profits from tobacco sales, the farmers began to build **plantations**, or large farms, to grow even more tobacco.

The plantation owners took over more and more land. They forced Indian families to

Tobacco was an important crop for early Marylanders.

leave their homes in Maryland. Some Indians moved first to the colonies of Pennsylvania and New York and finally to Canada. Other Indians stayed in Maryland, but many of them died from diseases brought by the colonists. By 1750 almost no Indians remained in Maryland.

The *Peggy Stewart,* carrying 2,000 pounds of British tea, burns in the harbor at Annapolis.

Great Britain wasn't the only European nation to send settlers to North America. France founded colonies, too. In the mid-1700s, France and Great Britain fought for control of the land around the **Great Lakes**. This conflict was called the French and Indian War, because many Indians sided with the French.

To pay for the war, the British government taxed sugar, tea, newspapers, playing cards, and other goods that the colonists bought from Britain. The settlers were angry. They bought as little as they could from Britain. The British government dropped some of the taxes but continued to tax tea. In protest, Marylanders burned the British ship *Peggy Stewart* and its cargo of tea in Annapolis.

The settlers wanted freedom from British rule so they could make their own laws. So soldiers from each of the 13 American colonies formed the Continental army. In 1775 the Americans went to war with the British. The conflict was called the War of Independence, or the American Revolution.

Very little fighting took place in Maryland during the Revolution. But the colony sent a group of soldiers, called the Maryland Line, to join the Continental army. In battles against the British, the Maryland Line was rarely beaten. One of Maryland's nicknames, the Old Line State, comes from the colony's dependable troops.

A soldier of the
Maryland Line

A sculpture of George Washington stands in the Maryland State House in Annapolis, where he signed the Treaty of Paris, ending the American Revolution.

On July 3, 1776, the people of Maryland declared that their colony was independent of Great Britain. The next day, representatives from all 13 colonies gathered to sign the Declaration of Independence. This document announced that the colonies no longer belonged to Britain. Four Marylanders signed the declaration.

Even after the colonies declared their independence, the war with Britain continued. Britain finally lost the war in 1783. Afterward, the former colonies agreed to create one nation, the United States of America. From late 1783 to mid-1784, the country's new Congress met in Annapolis at the Maryland State House. There, Congress ratified the Treaty of Paris, a document that officially ended the Revolutionary War.

On April 28, 1788, Maryland became the seventh state to join the United States. Three years later, Maryland gave the new nation land for a capital city—Washington, D.C.

Not long after the Revolution, the United States and Britain fought the War of 1812. Some American ships had been delivering goods to France, Britain's enemy. To prevent the goods from reaching the French, the British captured the American ships and forced 10,000 U.S. sailors to join the British navy.

Prior to the War of 1812, captured American sailors were forced to join the British navy.

The flag that inspired Francis Scott Key's poem "The Star-Spangled Banner" now hangs in the Smithsonian Institution *(above)*. This painting depicts Key's moment of inspiration *(right)*.

A Key Night in Baltimore

During the War of 1812, many fierce battles took place. At 7:00 A.M. on September 13, 1814, in the pouring rain, the British opened fire on Fort McHenry. The *Terror,* the *Volcano,* and 14 other warships hurled 200-pound bombs at the fort all day and long into the following night.

Francis Scott Key, a lawyer from Maryland, watched the bombardment from on board a ship. In the rain and dark, he couldn't tell who was winning the battle. But the next morning, an American flag was still flying high over the fort. Key knew then that the British hadn't captured Baltimore.

On the back of an old letter he had in his pocket, Key wrote a poem describing what he had seen. His poem, "The Star-Spangled Banner," later became the national anthem of the United States.

The United States launched an attack against British territory in Canada and against British ships at sea. In 1814 the British attacked Washington, D.C., and planned to invade Baltimore, Maryland's largest town.

The people of Baltimore were ready. They had strengthened Fort McHenry, a star-shaped fort that guarded Baltimore's harbor. Merchants even sank their own ships in the harbor to block British ships from the city. When the Battle of Baltimore was over, the city still belonged to Maryland.

The attack on Fort McHenry

The Baltimore Turnpike *(left)*, Chesapeake and Ohio Canal *(center)*, and Baltimore and Ohio Railroad *(right)*

Travel by River and Rail

In the early 1800s, Maryland was part of a growing transportation network. The Baltimore Turnpike was part of the National Road, which eventually reached from Washington, D.C., to St. Louis, Missouri. The Chesapeake and Ohio Canal, started in 1828, was built to connect the Potomac and Ohio Rivers, but the canal was never completed. Along the finished sections, mules towed boats loaded with crops and other goods. Also in 1828, the nation's first railroad, the Baltimore and Ohio, started laying tracks west from Baltimore. One of the first trains was a steam locomotive with finely decorated coaches.

The war ended in 1814. Afterward, Marylanders began building new roads, railroads, and canals. Travel and trade increased. In the 1820s, Marylanders begin building the Baltimore and Ohio (B&O) Railroad, one of the first railroads in the United States. Construction also began on the Chesapeake and Ohio (C&O) Canal.

Wealthy Marylanders continued to raise tobacco on big **plantations.** Slaves, mostly from Africa, did most of the farm work. But most Marylanders did not own plantations. Many were farmers who had only small plots of land. They plowed their own fields and planted their own crops. They did not own slaves.

Other Marylanders did not work on farms at all. In the Appalachian Mountains, some Marylanders dug coal.

In the 1800s, coal miners began digging coal out of the mountains in western Maryland.

In Baltimore, people sewed clothes, laid railroad tracks, and held other jobs.

Over the years, the Northern and Southern states disagreed about slavery and many other issues. The Northern states eventually outlawed slavery, and they wanted the Southern states to do the same. But politicians in the South refused. They argued that without slaves, plantation owners could not make a profit.

In 1861 some Southern states decided to form their own country, the Confederate States of America, also called the Confederacy. In the Confederacy, slavery was legal. The Northern states, called the Union, went to war to keep the South from breaking away from the United States. This conflict was called the Civil War.

Maryland was caught in the middle during the war. Many Marylanders supported the Southern states. Other people in Maryland supported the North.

The states of Virginia and Maryland surrounded Washington, D.C., the U.S. capital. Virginia had joined the Confederacy. If Maryland joined too, Washington, D.C., would be fenced in by Confederate states. The Union army stationed troops throughout Maryland and the U.S. capital. Pressured by the presence of Union soldiers, Maryland remained in the Union during the war. But some Maryland men fought for the Confederacy anyway.

During the Civil War, some slaves fled from the South to Maryland, a Union state.

Maryland's Antietam Creek was the site of a famous Civil War battle.

One of the bloodiest battles in U.S. history was fought in 1862 at Antietam Creek near Sharpsburg, Maryland. In one day, more than 23,000 soldiers were wounded or killed before the North claimed victory in the battle. Shortly after the Battle of Antietam, President Abraham Lincoln declared that all Southern slaves were free.

The war continued until 1865, when the

Confederacy surrendered. Afterward, many freed slaves moved to Maryland and other states that had sided with the Union. In Baltimore hundreds of schools were set up to teach former slaves, most of whom had never received an education. The students learned to read and write and then took jobs as factory workers or farmhands.

After the Civil War, Baltimore became a center for business, education, and the arts. The Peabody Conservatory of Music (later called the Peabody Institute) had been opened before the war, in 1857. Johns Hopkins University began operating in 1876. The Enoch Pratt Free Library, one of the first public libraries in the United States, was founded in 1886.

This photograph of president Abraham Lincoln *(center)* was taken just after the battle of Antietam.

In the early 1900s, the oyster industry thrived along the Chesapeake Bay. Boats brought oysters to the docks *(right),* then workers shucked the oysters *(above left)* and canned them *(above right).*

During the early 1900s, industry in Maryland continued to thrive. Workers in Baltimore's factories produced cloth and canned oysters. The city became famous for producing straw hats. The B&O Railroad carried trainloads of Baltimore's products westward to be sold in other states.

But business activity was disrupted in 1904, when a big fire spread through downtown Baltimore. The fire burned for two days and destroyed almost all the downtown buildings. No lives were lost, but the fire caused about $100 million in damage.

Fire raged through downtown Baltimore in 1904, destroying most of the city.

During World War II, Marylanders built huge warships for the military.

Maryland's industries played an important role during wartime. During World War I (1914–1918), Marylanders built ships and airplanes and sewed thousands of uniforms for the military. During World War II (1939–1945), mapmakers in Maryland made more than 30,000 maps to help the U.S. military plan for battle. Factories made more ships and airplanes for the armed forces. The state's population grew rapidly as people from other parts of the country came to work in Maryland's factories.

As new businesses and more people came to Maryland, the state added new transportation facilities, including bridges, tunnels, and expressways. The Friendship International Airport (later called Baltimore-Washington International Airport) opened in 1950. The U.S. government, based in nearby Washington, D.C., also established many important research centers in Maryland. For instance, the Goddard Space Flight Center was opened in the city of Greenbelt in 1959.

Many of Maryland's citizens were African Americans. They had gained some freedoms since the Civil War, but some white people still treated blacks unfairly. During the 1950s and 1960s, African Americans tried to gain the same rights that white people had. In Maryland and other states, black people protested against unfair laws. This effort was known as the **civil rights movement**. Cambridge, Maryland, was the site of heated civil rights protests in the summer of 1963.

Demonstrators pray together at a civil rights meeting in Cambridge, Maryland, in 1963.

In the late 1900s, Maryland began to face new problems. For instance, downtown Baltimore became run-down. Crime and poverty increased. Many people and businesses left downtown for suburban areas. To help bring visitors, businesses, and residents back to the city center, Baltimore began to revitalize its Inner Harbor area. Many old buildings were restored and new attractions were opened, including the National Aquarium. In the 1980s, Maryland also began a program to clean up pollution in the Chesapeake Bay.

Baltimore's revitalized Inner Harbor is now home to many popular tourist attractions.

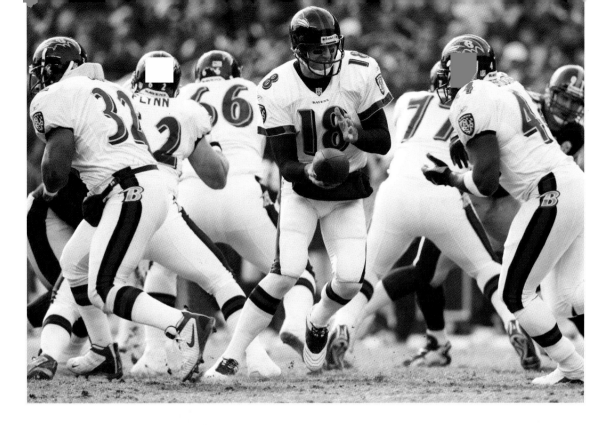

In 2001 Marylanders found a new reason to celebrate when their pro football team, the Baltimore Ravens, won Super Bowl XXXV, beating the New York Giants. From sports to business to the environment, Marylanders are working together to make their state a better place to live. They want to keep Maryland beautiful and prosperous for many years to come.

The Baltimore Ravens football team won the 2001 Super Bowl, defeating the New York Giants.

Master sandcastle builders have transformed this Maryland beach into a work of art.

PEOPLE & ECONOMY

America in Miniature

ecause Maryland is so diverse—with big cities, little towns, and wilderness areas all close together in one small state—it is often called America in Miniature. More than 5 million people call Maryland home. Maryland's most populated cities and suburbs—Baltimore, Columbia, Silver Spring, and Dundalk—are located in a crowded stretch of land that runs from Baltimore to Washington, D.C. About 80 percent of Maryland's residents live within this strip.

Many Marylanders have European ancestors. In the 1700s and 1800s, most Maryland-bound **immigrants** (newcomers) arrived by boat from Great Britain and Germany. In the late 1800s, many Italian, Russian, and Polish people settled in Baltimore.

At Baltimore's AFRAM EXPO, girls celebrate their African heritage with baskets and colorful costumes.

Many of these people lived together in neighborhoods with others from the same home country.

Since the 1960s, many Spanish-speaking immigrants have arrived in Maryland from Central American countries such as El Salvador. More than 27 percent of Maryland's residents are African Americans. Asian Americans make up 4 percent of the state's population. Less than 1 percent of Maryland's population is Native American. Most are descendants of Indians who lived by the Chesapeake Bay in the 1600s.

Baltimore is the artistic and historic center of the state. It has interesting old neighborhoods, museums, theaters, and historical sites. But Maryland's past can be found in almost every city and town.

Baltimore attracts nearly 13 million visitors each year.

In Saint Michaels, history buffs can stop by the Chesapeake Bay Maritime Museum to learn about people and ships that have sailed the bay. In central and western Maryland, visitors can tour Civil War battlefields. They can see famous homes and buildings that once hosted presidents George Washington and Abraham Lincoln.

Annapolis, the state capital, features a historic capitol building, the Maryland State House. It has been in use for more than 200 years—longer than any other capitol building in the nation. Many houses in Annapolis are also quite old. They were built before the Revolutionary War.

In fall, Marylanders cheer for the Baltimore Ravens, Super Bowl champs in 2001. During summer, Marylanders watch the Baltimore Orioles swat baseballs at Oriole Park in Camden Yards. Many people sail boats on the Chesapeake Bay. Others fish in the streams and lakes of western Maryland.

The Baltimore Orioles are named after Maryland's state bird.

A neck-and-neck finish at the Preakness Stakes

In winter, skiers wind down the slopes of the Appalachian Mountains.

Each May, at the Pimlico Race Course, select Thoroughbred horses compete in the Preakness Stakes, one of the most famous horse races in the world. Other races aren't so serious. The Hard Crab Derby is held every September in Crisfield. Onlookers wonder whose blue crab will make it across the finish line first!

Students at the U.S. Naval Academy stand at attention during a military drill.

Education has been important in Maryland since colonial days. Saint John's College, which is more than 300 years old, was Maryland's first public, or free, school. The Peabody Institute, the nation's oldest music school, is part of Johns Hopkins University. The U.S. Naval Academy in Annapolis has trained students to become naval officers since before the Civil War.

Almost 70 percent of Maryland's workers hold service jobs. They include doctors and nurses, salespeople, and office workers.

Another 17 percent of Maryland's population works for the government. Some people work for the state government in Annapolis, the capital city. Other Marylanders work for the U.S. government in Washington, D.C. They hold jobs at the Smithsonian Institution, the Department of Defense, and other government offices.

Many U.S. government research centers—such as the National Institutes of Health, Goddard Space Flight Center, and National Agricultural Research Center—are located in Maryland. The scientists who work at these centers study everything from human diseases to insects.

At the National Agricultural Research Center, scientists study how air pollution affects crops.

In Baltimore, Cumberland, Hagerstown, and other cities in Maryland, factories hire people to make steel, build ships, and produce gasoline. Other workers sew clothing, process sugar, or work at printing companies. Some residents of the Eastern Shore pack frozen seafood and vegetables into cans. Manufacturing employs about 7 percent of Maryland's workforce.

Workers at a food processing plant pack cucumbers into cans.

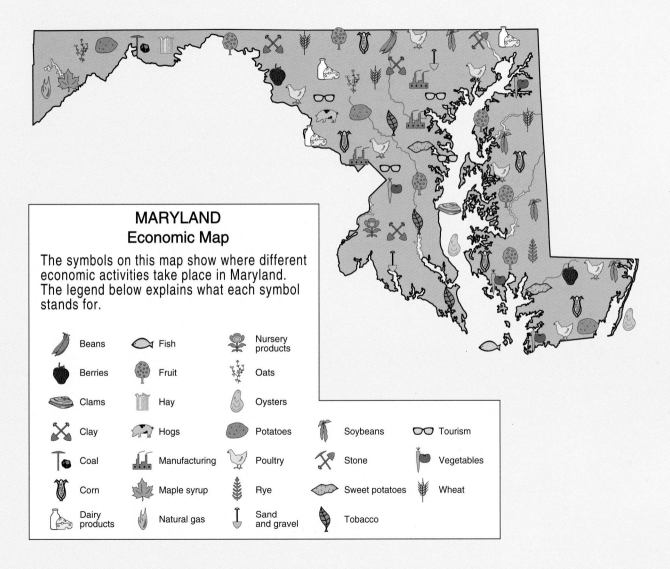

MARYLAND
Economic Map

The symbols on this map show where different economic activities take place in Maryland. The legend below explains what each symbol stands for.

Beans	Fish	Nursery products		
Berries	Fruit	Oats		
Clams	Hay	Oysters		
Clay	Hogs	Potatoes	Soybeans	Tourism
Coal	Manufacturing	Poultry	Stone	Vegetables
Corn	Maple syrup	Rye	Sweet potatoes	Wheat
Dairy products	Natural gas	Sand and gravel	Tobacco	

49

Peaches and other kinds of fruit grow in western Maryland.

More Marylanders work in factories or offices than on farms, but agriculture is still important to Maryland. On the Eastern Shore, farmers grow vegetables. They also raise chickens in long, low buildings called poultry houses. Tobacco farming still thrives in southern Maryland. In the western part of the state, farmers raise cows, tend fruit orchards, and tap maple trees for syrup.

Coal is a major resource in western Maryland. Miners dig the coal out of huge pits called strip mines. The coal is then used to heat homes and businesses. In other parts of the state, workers mine limestone, sand, and gravel, which are used to make roads and buildings.

Skipjacks are still used to harvest oysters from Chesapeake Bay.

Boats of the Bay

Over the centuries, creative Marylanders have built many different kinds of boats. Some of these boats were designed especially for gathering oysters in Chesapeake Bay.

Native Americans were the first ones to gather oysters from the bay. They fished from canoes made of hollowed-out logs. British settlers gathered oysters from sailboats, which could travel more swiftly than canoes. One kind of sailboat had three sails and a flat bottom. It was called a brogan.

In the 1860s, **watermen** (people who make a living by fishing) began using dredges—big iron rakes—to scrape oysters from the bottom of the bay. To pull the heavy dredges over the oyster beds, watermen needed a more powerful boat. The brogan was made bigger and stronger. No one knows exactly why, but this new kind of boat was called a bugeye.

The skipjack was developed in the early 1890s. Like the bugeye, the skipjack was made for oyster dredging. But it was smaller and simpler than the bugeye, and it was cheaper to build.

By law, watermen must use sailboats—not motorboats—to dredge oysters from the bay. So graceful skipjacks still sail in Maryland, dragging their dredges behind them.

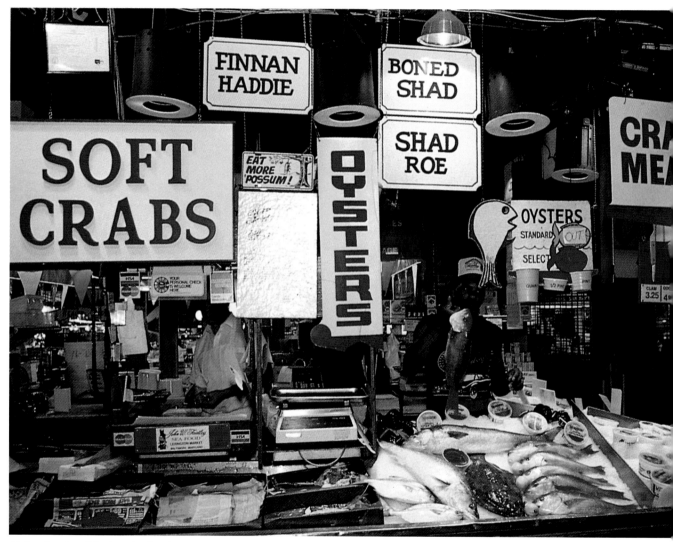

At Lexington Market in Baltimore, shoppers can buy all kinds of seafood.

Chesapeake Bay is a great place for sailing.

When many people think of Maryland, they think about fishing on the Chesapeake Bay. Fishing crews on the bay catch blue crabs, clams, striped bass (called rock-fish in Maryland), bluefin tuna, and flounder by the ton. They also dredge the water for oysters.

THE ENVIRONMENT

Keeping the Bay Clean

any Marylanders live near one of their state's most famous natural features, the Chesapeake Bay. The bay is an **estuary**—a place where a river and an ocean meet. Fresh river water and salty ocean water mix in the Chesapeake Bay, the largest estuary in the United States.

The Chesapeake Bay is deep in some places and shallow in others. The mixture of freshwater and saltwater in the shallow areas once made the bay a perfect home for

Pollution has hurt hermit crabs and other Chesapeake Bay animals.

more than 2,700 different kinds of plants and animals. But the bay is not as perfect a home as it once was.

Over the years, many **pollutants**, or harmful wastes, have entered the bay. Nitrogen and phosphorus are two of these pollutants. These substances are used to make many products, including household soaps and lawn and garden fertilizers. After people wash with soap or treat their lawns with fertilizers, nitrogen and phosphorus run into sewage pipes and then into rivers that drain into the bay. More nitrogen and phosphorus enter the bay from sewage treatment plants.

People who rely on catching seafood for a living are also hurt by pollution.

Rain washes fertilizers from farmland into nearby rivers, which eventually flow to the bay.

Too much nitrogen and phosphorus cause algae to bloom, or grow very rapidly. Algae are plants that grow in the water. So much nitrogen and phosphorus have entered Chesapeake Bay that thick mats of algae float near the water's surface.

These mats prevent sunlight from reaching plants on the bottom of the bay. Without enough sunlight, the plants die. The fish that eat the plants also lose an important source of food. In addition, when algae die and decay, oxygen levels in the water drop, leaving less oxygen for animals in the water. Many sea animals eventually leave the bay or die.

Factories release **toxic waste** into the bay, including chemicals and poisonous metals like lead and mercury. Factories also release pollution into the air through smokestacks. The pollution mixes with rain and then falls into streams and rivers, some of which flow into the bay. Household items like paint, oil, and gasoline also pollute the bay.

Pollution in Chesapeake Bay has poisoned many plants and animals, including fish. Birds, such as bald eagles and osprey, that have eaten the poisoned fish have gotten sick too. People can also get sick if they eat poisoned fish from the bay.

Sediment, or loose soil, is another problem for Chesapeake Bay. When people cut down trees to clear land for construction, the soil gets loose and crumbly. Rainwater washes the soil into nearby creeks, rivers, and marshes. These eventually flow into Chesapeake Bay. The sediment clouds the bay's waters, fills its channels, and smothers its plants and animals.

In the 1960s, a group of Baltimore citizens decided that it was time to clean up the bay. They formed the Chesapeake Bay Foundation (CBF) in 1967. Over the years, CBF has worked with representatives from Delaware, Virginia, Pennsylvania, Washington, D.C., and the U.S. government to try to protect the bay. The group has fought for new laws and programs to help keep the bay clean.

Factories have helped out by agreeing to cut down on pollution and toxic waste. Scientists have also helped by researching ways to reduce nitrogen and phosphorus in wastewater. Other scientists have tried to save the animals that live in the bay. They've even moved oysters and fish from polluted parts of the bay into cleaner waters.

The government has also helped by setting up wildlife preserves around the bay. These lands are set aside for plants and animals only. People can't harm them by building houses, roads, or factories there. In 2000 the governors of Maryland and other states around the bay signed the Chesapeake Bay Agreement, setting up new guidelines for

protecting and restoring the bay.

The CBF has worked hard to educate people about the importance of keeping the bay clean. By 2001 the foundation had 16 educational centers and more than 80,000 members. The work is not done—the bay still suffers from pollution. But the more people who get involved, the better the chances for success.

Marylanders are working together to keep Chesapeake Bay clean.

Fun Facts

Wye Mills, Maryland, boasts the largest white oak tree in the United States. More than 400 years old, the Wye Oak is taller than a 10-story building.

The first umbrella factory in the United States opened in Baltimore in 1828. Its slogan was "Born in Baltimore, raised everywhere."

You can walk across Maryland in less than 30 minutes! The state is only 1.5 miles wide at its narrowest point.

The Wye Oak

The first successful hot-air balloon flight in the United States was launched in Maryland in 1784. The balloon carried 13-year-old Edward Warren of Baltimore.

In 1830 the Baltimore and Ohio (B&O) Railroad, which was founded in Maryland, operated the first passenger train in the United States. The train could travel up to 20 miles per hour.

Maryland's official state sport is jousting. In this sport, a contestant mounted on horseback tries to pick up a ring with the end of a long lance, or spear. Each year, Maryland holds a state jousting tournament.

The first bookmobile in the United States began operation at the Washington County Free Library in April 1907.

STATE SONG

Maryland's state song was written during the Civil War by a Louisiana teacher named James Ryder Randall. Randall wrote the song after learning that Union troops had marched through Baltimore.

MARYLAND, MY MARYLAND

Words by James Ryder Randall; music traditional

The des-pot's heel is on thy shore, Ma-ry-land, My Ma-ry-land! His

torch is at thy tem-ple door, Ma-ry-land, My Ma-ry-land, A-

venge the pa-tri-ot-ic gore That fleck'd the streets of Bal-ti-more, And

be the Bat-tle Queen of yore, Ma-ry-land, My Ma-ry-land!

A MARYLAND RECIPE

Maryland is famous for its seafood.
Crabs, oysters, shrimps, and clams all
live in the Chesapeake Bay. Over the years,
Marylanders have created many tasty recipes
using the seafood they catch in the bay.
This casserole contains both crab and shrimp.

BAKED ANNAPOLIS SEAFOOD CASSEROLE

1 pound crab meat
1 pound whole shrimp
1 cup mayonnaise
½ cup green pepper, chopped
¼ cup onion, chopped

1½ cups celery, chopped
½ teaspoon salt
1 tablespoon Worcestershire sauce
2 cups potato chips, crushed
paprika

1. Ask an adult to preheat oven to 400° F.
2. In large bowl, combine all ingredients, except potato chips and paprika.
3. Pour mixture into 2.5-quart casserole dish.
4. Top with crushed potato chips and sprinkle with paprika.
5. With an adult's help, bake casserole in oven for 20 to 25 minutes.

Makes 8 servings.

HISTORICAL TIMELINE

8000 B.C.   Native Americans arrive in Maryland.

A.D. 1632   King Charles I of England grants the Maryland region to Lord Baltimore.

1634   Colonists begin building Saint Mary's City.

1649   Maryland passes a religious tolerance law.

1775   The Maryland Line joins the Continental army.

1776   Maryland and the other American colonies declare independence from Britain.

1788   Maryland becomes the seventh state in the United States.

1791   Maryland gives the nation land for its capital, Washington, D.C.

1814   During the War of 1812 (1812–1814), American forces repel a British attack on Fort McHenry; Francis Scott Key writes "The Star-Spangled Banner."

1828   Marylanders begin building the Baltimore and Ohio Railroad and the Chesapeake and Ohio Canal.

1845 The U.S. Naval Academy is founded at Annapolis.

1862 Union troops defeat Confederates at the Battle of Antietam near Sharpsburg.

1876 Johns Hopkins University is founded in Baltimore.

1904 Fire destroys most of downtown Baltimore.

1938 The National Institutes of Health moves to offices in Bethesda.

1940s Thousands of workers from the South and Appalachia come to Maryland to work in defense plants.

1959 Goddard Space Flight Center opens in Greenbelt.

1967 Baltimore citizens establish the Chesapeake Bay Foundation.

1981 The National Aquarium opens on Baltimore's Inner Harbor.

2000 The Chesapeake Bay Agreement establishes new guidelines for protecting Chesapeake Bay.

2001 The Baltimore Ravens win Super Bowl XXXV.

OUTSTANDING MARYLANDERS

Benjamin Banneker

Benjamin Banneker (1731–1806), an African American, was born near Baltimore County. He taught himself mathematics and astronomy and went on to become a surveyor for the U.S. government. In this job, Banneker helped lay out the boundaries for Washington, D.C. He also published several almanacs—books that included weather predictions for the upcoming year.

Tom Clancy

Eubie Blake (1883–1983) was born in Baltimore. A pioneer of ragtime music, Blake wrote "I'm Just Wild about Harry" and "Memories of You," songs that were popular in the early 1900s.

Tom Clancy (born 1947), a popular American writer, was born in Baltimore. He attended Baltimore's Loyola College. His novels deal with international spies and military secrets. One of Clancy's most famous novels is *The Hunt for Red October* (1984), which was made into a movie in 1990.

Frederick Douglass

Frederick Douglass (1818–1895) was born a slave in Tuckahoe, Maryland. As a young man, he escaped from his master. Douglass spent the rest of life protesting slavery. He started an antislavery newspaper called the *North Star* and spoke with President Abraham Lincoln about the evils of slavery.

Mama Cass Elliot

Mama Cass Elliot (1941–1974) was born Ellen Naomi Cohen in Baltimore. She was a member of the 1960s folk group the Mamas and Papas. The group recorded many hit songs, including "California Dreamin'" and "Monday, Monday."

Philip Glass (born 1937) is an innovative American composer. He helped develop a musical style called minimalism, which features short repeated patterns and simple harmonies. His work also includes elements of rock 'n' roll, African, Indian, and classical music. Glass was born in Baltimore.

Frances Ellen Watkins Harper (1825–1911), an author and public speaker, began writing poetry as a teenager. She spoke out against slavery and rallied for women's rights. Born in Baltimore, Harper was the first black person in the United States to have a short story published.

Matthew Henson

Matthew Henson (1867–1955) was an African American explorer. Born on a small farm in Charles County, he accompanied Robert E. Peary on the first expedition to the North Pole in 1909. Although Peary received credit as the first person to reach the pole, many people believe that Henson arrived there before him.

Billie Holiday

Billie Holiday (1915–1959), from Baltimore, was one of the most popular singers in jazz history. In 1927 Holiday moved to New York, where she began singing in clubs and recording music. Her style has influenced many other singers.

Johns Hopkins (1795–1873) grew up in Anne Arundel County. He helped create the B&O Railroad. At his death, Hopkins left $7 million to build the Johns Hopkins University and Johns Hopkins Hospital.

Johns Hopkins

Francis Scott Key (1779–1843) was born in Frederick County. Key, a lawyer, witnessed the bombardment of Fort McHenry during the War of 1812. The next day, he wrote a poem about the battle. He then set it to music, borrowing the tune from a popular English song. His song, "The Star-Spangled Banner," became the national anthem of the United States in 1931.

Francis Scott Key

Barry Levinson

Thurgood Marshall

H.L. Mencken

Kweisi Mfume

Barry Levinson (born 1942), a successful Hollywood producer, director, and writer, was born in Baltimore. Some of his most famous films include *Diner* (1982), *Good Morning, Vietnam* (1987), and *Rain Man* (1988).

Thurgood Marshall (1908–1993), a native of Baltimore, graduated at the head of his law school class at Howard University in Washington, D.C. As a lawyer, Marshall argued and won court cases that gave black people more civil rights. In 1967 Marshall became the first black judge to sit on the U.S. Supreme Court.

H. L. Mencken (1880–1956), born in Baltimore, wrote humorous stories, essays, and articles about Americans. His work appeared in many publications, including the magazines *Smart Set* and *American Mercury*. Mencken's most famous book, *The American Language* (1919), examined the English language in the United States.

Kweisi Mfume (born 1948) was born Frizzell Gray in Baltimore. He later adopted an African name, which means "conquering son of kings." Mfume served in the U.S. House of Representatives for almost 10 years. A Democrat, he often worked on behalf of African Americans and the poor. Since 1996 Mfume has served as president of the National Association for the Advancement of Colored People (NAACP).

Charles Willson Peale (1741–1827), born in Queen Anne's County, was an acclaimed American painter. He painted portraits of some of the most prominent figures in American history, including George and Martha Washington, Benjamin Franklin, and Thomas Jefferson. Many of Peale's 17 children also became painters.

Cal Ripken Jr. (born 1960) is one of baseball's finest shortstops. He holds the record for the most consecutive games played by a major leaguer—2,632 games. Ripken played his entire career with the Baltimore Orioles. He was born in Havre de Grace.

Francis Peyton Rous

Francis Peyton Rous (1879–1970) was born in Baltimore. He studied chicken viruses, and his work has helped in modern cancer research. For his discoveries, Rous won the 1966 Nobel Prize in medicine.

George "Babe" Ruth (1895–1948) has been called the most famous person in American sports history. Born in Baltimore, Ruth began his baseball career at age 19 with Baltimore's minor-league team. Ruth went on to play for the New York Yankees. He was known for his powerful home run hitting.

"Babe" Ruth

Upton Sinclair (1878–1968), born in Baltimore, wrote at least 90 books, hundreds of articles, and many plays. One of Sinclair's best-known novels, *The Jungle*, brought attention to some of the nation's social problems, including the difficult lives of factory workers in the early 1900s.

Upton Sinclair

Harriet Tubman (1821–1913), from Bucktown, escaped from slavery and fled to the North when she was about 28 years old. Tubman returned to the South 19 times, risking her life to lead more than 300 slaves to freedom.

Leon Uris (born 1924), from Baltimore, is a writer most famous for his novel *Exodus*, which tells the story of the Jewish migration to Israel. His other books include *Mila 18* and *Trinity*.

Harriet Tubman

FACTS-AT-A-GLANCE

Nickname: Old Line State

Song: "Maryland, My Maryland"

Motto: Fatti Maschii Parole Femine
(Manly Deeds, Womanly Words)

Flower: black-eyed Susan

Tree: white oak

Bird: Baltimore oriole

Boat: skipjack

Dog: Chesapeake Bay retriever

Drink: milk

Sport: jousting

Date and ranking of statehood: April 28,
1788; the seventh state

Capital: Annapolis

Area: 9,775 square miles

Rank in area, nationwide: 42nd

Average January temperature: 33° F

Average July temperature: 75° F

Maryland's state flag, adopted in 1904, contains the coats of arms of Lord Baltimore's ancestors—the Calverts on his father's side and Crosslands on his mother's side. The black-and-gold sections show the Calvert arms, while the red-and-white sections represent the Crosslands.

POPULATION GROWTH

Millions

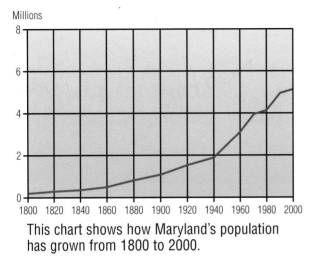

This chart shows how Maryland's population has grown from 1800 to 2000.

Maryland's state seal shows a farmer, a fisher, and a shield with the Calvert and Crossland coats of arms. The date 1632, the year King Charles I granted Maryland to Lord Baltimore, also appears on the seal. The reverse side of the seal shows Lord Baltimore dressed as a knight in armor.

Population: 5,296,486 (2000 census)

Rank in population, nationwide: 19th

Major cities and populations: (2000 census) Baltimore (651,154), Columbia (88,254), Silver Spring (76,540), Dundalk (62,306)

U.S. senators: 2

U.S. representatives: 8

Electoral votes: 10

Natural resources: coal, granite, gravel, limestone, loam and clay soils, natural gas, sand, talc

Agricultural products: apples, beef cattle, chickens, corn, cucumbers, maple syrup, milk, snap beans, soybeans, tobacco, tomatoes

Fishing industry: Atlantic croakers, blue crabs, bluefish, catfish, clams, crabs, menhaden, striped bass, white perch

Manufactured goods: electrical machinery, fertilizers, food products, metals, paint, printed materials, soap, transportation equipment

WHERE MARYLANDERS WORK

Services—68 percent (services include jobs in trade; community, social, and personal services; finance, insurance, and real estate; transportation, communication, and utilities)

Government—17 percent

Manufacturing—7 percent

Construction—6 percent

Agriculture—2 percent

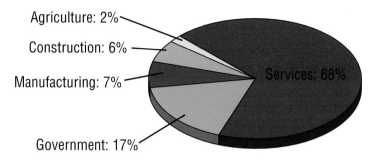

Agriculture: 2%
Construction: 6%
Manufacturing: 7%
Services: 68%
Government: 17%

GROSS STATE PRODUCT

Services—67 percent

Government—18 percent

Manufacturing—9 percent

Construction—5 percent

Agriculture—1 percent

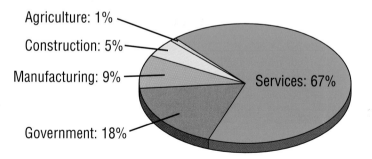

Agriculture: 1%
Construction: 5%
Manufacturing: 9%
Services: 67%
Government: 18%

MARYLAND WILDLIFE

Mammals: chipmunk, eastern cottontail rabbit, gray fox, mink, opossum, otter, raccoon, red fox, squirrel, white-tailed deer, woodchuck

Birds: duck, goose, grouse, partridge, wild turkey, woodcock

Amphibians and reptiles: diamondback terrapin, salamander, skink, snake, toad, tree frog, turtle

Fish: alewife, bluefish, carp, catfish, clams, crab, croaker, menhaden, oyster, shrimp, striped bass, trout

Trees: ash, bald cypress, beech, hemlock, hickory, laurel, loblolly pine, maple, Spanish oak, sweet gum, tupelo, white oak, white pine

Wild plants: azalea, black-eyed Susan, blackberry, dewberry, raspberry, rhododendron, sedge, strawberry

Opossum mothers carry their babies on their backs *(above top)*. Wild turkeys roam the Maryland woods *(above)*.

PLACES TO VISIT

Antietam National Battlefield, Sharpsburg
Visitors can tour the scene of one of the bloodiest battles of the Civil War. The site also includes a museum, theater, bookstore, and research library.

B&O Railroad Museum, Baltimore
The museum teaches about the history of American railroading through exhibits, educational programs, and special events. Exhibits focus on the B&O and other early American railroads.

Babe Ruth Birthplace and Museum, Baltimore
Visitors will learn about baseball legend Babe Ruth's life and career, as well as the history of the Baltimore Orioles baseball team. The museum contains the restored house where Ruth was born, plus nearby exhibits.

Banneker Douglass Museum, Annapolis
Named for African American pioneers Benjamin Banneker and Frederick Douglass, this museum is dedicated to preserving Maryland's African American heritage.

Fort McHenry National Monument, Baltimore
Visitors will learn about the Battle of Baltimore, which inspired Francis Scott Key to write "The Star-Spangled Banner." The fort offers tours, exhibits, and educational programs for visitors.

Goddard Space Flight Center Visitor Center, Greenbelt

At NASA's Goddard Space Flight Center, scientists study and share knowledge about the planets, the stars, and the universe. At Goddard's visitor center, people can learn all about space exploration through hands-on exhibits, tours, and special programs.

Historic Saint Mary's City, Saint Mary's City

Established in 1634, Saint Mary's City was Maryland's first colonial settlement. The historic village contains a museum; a replica of the *Maryland Dove*, Lord Baltimore's ship; a re-created tobacco plantation; and re-created buildings from the 1600s.

Maryland Science Center, Baltimore

Science comes to life at this big Inner Harbor museum. Facilities include educational exhibits, an IMAX theater, and the Davis Planetarium.

National Aquarium, Baltimore

The aquarium contains thousands of fish, reptiles, and birds in various habitats, including a tropical rain forest and an Atlantic coral reef.

U.S. Naval Academy Visitor Center, Annapolis

The visitor center offers displays, interactive exhibits, and a film about the U.S. Naval Academy. Visitors can also take a guided walking tour of the campus.

USS *Constellation*, Baltimore

One of the first U.S. warships, the *Constellation* was built in 1797. It later became a museum, docked in Baltimore's Inner Harbor. Visitors can tour the ship and learn about naval history.

ANNUAL EVENTS

Greater Baltimore-Washington Marble Show, Baltimore—*March*

Maryland International Kite Festival, Ocean City—*April*

Preakness Stakes, Baltimore—*May*

Boat Bumm's International Cardboard Boat Race, Oxford—*June*

Hard Crab Derby, Crisfield—*August–September*

Skipjack Race and Festival, Deal Island—*September*

AFRAM EXPO, Baltimore—*September*

Maryland Seafood Festival, Annapolis—*September*

Star-Spangled Banner Weekend, Baltimore—*September*

Chocolate Festival, Baltimore—*October*

Oysterfest, Saint Michaels—*November*

LEARN MORE ABOUT MARYLAND

BOOKS

General

Burgan, Michael. *Maryland.* Danbury, CT: Children's Press, 1999. For older readers.

Fradin, Dennis Brindell. *Maryland.* Chicago: Children's Press, 1994.

Thompson, Kathleen. *Maryland.* Austin, TX: Raintree Steck-Vaughn, 1996.

Special Interest

Ferris, Jeri. *What Are You Figuring Now?: A Story about Benjamin Banneker.* Minneapolis: Carolrhoda Books, Inc., 1988. The story of Maryland's Benjamin Banneker, an accomplished black mathematician, astronomer, and surveyor, who helped lay out Washington, D.C., in 1791.

Reger, James. *The Battle of Antietam.* San Diego: Lucent Books, 1997. Sharpsburg, Maryland, was the site of one of the fiercest battles of the Civil War. This books explores the battle and tells about the soldiers and officers who fought there.

Spier, Peter. *The Star-Spangled Banner.* New York: Yearling Books, 1992. This award-winning book tells the story of the War of 1812 and the battle that inspired Francis Scott Key to write "The Star-Spangled Banner."

Weidt, Maryann N. *Matthew Henson.* Minneapolis: Lerner Publications Company, 2002. The story of Maryland-born Arctic explorer Mathew Henson. In 1909 Henson was a member of the first group of people to reach the North Pole.

Weidt, Maryann N. *Voice of Freedom: A Story about Frederick Douglass.* Minneapolis: Carolrhoda Books, Inc., 2001. Born a slave, Frederick Douglass went on to become an important leader in the American antislavery movement.

Fiction

Hahn, Mary Downing. *Anna All Year Round.* New York: William Morrow & Co., 2001. Anna, the daughter of German immigrants, grows up in Baltimore in the years before World War I. Her story is accompanied by vibrant black-and-white illustrations.

Rinaldi, Ann. *Amelia's War.* New York: Scholastic, Inc., 1999. The people of Hagerstown, Maryland, are divided in their loyalties during the Civil War. Twelve-year-old Amelia vows to remain neutral. But when a Confederate general threatens to burn the town, Amelia must take action.

WEBSITES

Maryland Electronic Capital
<http://www.mec.state.md.us>
The state of Maryland's official website contains information on state government, towns and cities, business, education, tourism, and more.

The Official Website of Maryland Tourism
<http://www.mdisfun.org>
People visiting Maryland will find lots of helpful information on this site. It includes sections on lodging, historic attractions, cultural events, festivals, shopping, dining, transportation, and more. A special Kids' Corner has lots of fun facts and games about Maryland.

The Baltimore Sun
<http://www.baltimoresun.com>
In print since 1837, the *Baltimore Sun* is one of the most famous newspapers in the United States. The paper's online edition includes sections on news, business, sports, and the arts, plus classified ads and other community information.

Maryland Historical Society
<http://www.mdhs.org>
Founded in 1844, the Maryland Historical Society is dedicated to preserving the state's history and heritage. The website offers information on the society's programs and facilities, which include a library, a museum, educational activities, and special events.

PRONUNCIATION GUIDE

Antietam (an-TEET-uhm)

Appalachian (ap-uh-LAY-chuhn)

Assateague (AS-uh-teeg)

Chesapeake (CHEHS-uh-peek)

Choptank (CHAHP-tangk)

Nanticoke (NAN-tih-kohk)

Patapsco (puh-TAP-skoh)

Piscataway (pihs-KAT-uh-way)

Pocomoke (POH-kuh-mohk)

Potomac (puh-TOH-mihk)

Susquehanna (suhs-kwuh-HAN-uh)

Wicomico (wy-KAHM-uh-koh)

Baltimore's Inner Harbor is a great spot for fun and relaxation.

GLOSSARY

civil rights movement: a movement to gain equal rights, or freedoms, for all citizens—regardless of race, religion, and sex

colony: a territory ruled by a country some distance away

estuary: an ocean inlet where fresh river water mixes with salty ocean water

Great Lakes: a chain of five big lakes in Canada and the northern United States. The lakes are named Superior, Michigan, Huron, Erie, and Ontario.

immigrant: a person who moves to a foreign country and settles there

marsh: a spongy wetland soaked with water for long periods. Marshes are usually treeless; grasses are the main forms of vegetation there.

plantation: a large farm that is also home to the farm owners and farm-workers. In the past, American plantation owners often used slave labor.

pollutant: a substance that dirties or poisons a natural resource, such as air or water

sediment: solid materials—such as soil, sand, or minerals—that are carried into a body of water by wind, ice, or running water

toxic waste: poisonous material that contaminates the environment and can cause death, disease, and other dangers

waterman: a person who earns his or her living by fishing, gathering shellfish, or working at another job on the water

INDEX

PHOTO ACKNOWLEDGMENTS